Underwat World

written by Jaclyn Crupi

Under the sea is a beautiful world full of plants and animals.

Some are very small and you have to look carefully to find them.

Others are enormous,
such as whales and some *seaweed*.

The ocean is home to lots of fish.
Some fish live in warm waters.
Others live where the water is cold.

Some fish are bright and colourful.
Fish can be many *shapes*.

An Arctic fish

Tropical fish

Puffer fish

Sailfish

Fish can be big and they can be small.

The whale shark is the biggest fish in the ocean.

The smallest fish in the ocean is smaller than a *pea*.

The stout infantfish is the smallest fish.

The whale shark is the biggest fish.

Turtles live in this underwater world, too.

They have a hard shell.

This shell is made up of *bones*.

Turtles are under the water for a lot of the time,
but they must come up to the top for *air*.

Turtles also spend some time on land, and this is where they lay their eggs. Some turtles live for a very long time.

It's not just fish and sea animals that live in the ocean.
Plants live there, too.
You can see lots of seaweed and *seagrass* under the sea.

In the ocean, there are tiny animals called *polyps*.
These animals stay in one place.
They build houses made of *limestone* around themselves.
We call these houses *coral*.

Seaweed and seagrass

Coral

Coral is very beautiful and has many colours.
Some coral is soft and some coral is hard.
Small fish like to hide in the coral
because it is a safe place.
They can also find food there.

Sharks are big fish that live in the ocean.
They have sharp teeth and very strong *jaws*.
Most sharks eat meat but some eat only plants.
Sharks are very good at smelling.
They can also see and hear very well.
Sharks can hear fish moving in the water
from a long way away.

Great white shark

Hammerhead shark

Bull shark

Tiger shark

11

Whales are the biggest animals in the ocean.

Many people think whales are fish, but they are not.

Whales need air like we do.

To take in air, they have a *blowhole* in the top of their head.

Some whales eat only small plants.

Some eat fish and other sea animals.

Whales swim by moving their tails up and down, and moving their fins (*flippers*).

Southern right whale

Killer whale

Blue whale

dorsal fin

blowhole

mouth

Humpback whale

tail

eye

fin

13

The underwater world is full of colourful plants
and animals.
When you *snorkel,* you can look down
and see this beautiful world.
Fish, turtles, coral, whales and sharks are all part of
the ocean; so are *starfish,* seaweed, *jellyfish* and *stingrays.*

We need to know as much as we can
about the animals and plants in the ocean.
Then we can take care of them
and their beautiful underwater world.

Jellyfish

Seaweed

Stingray

Starfish

Coral

Picture glossary

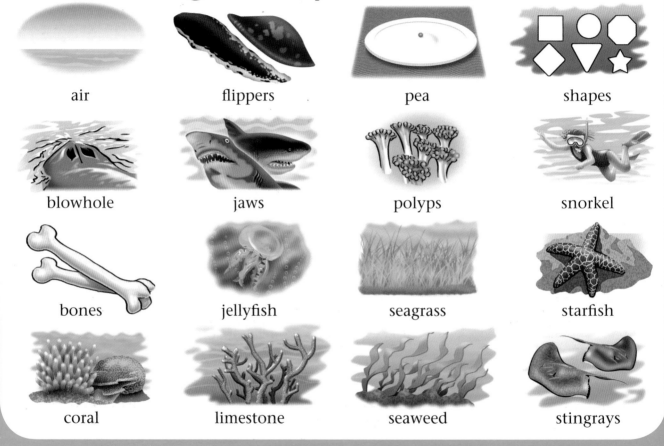

air

flippers

pea

shapes

blowhole

jaws

polyps

snorkel

bones

jellyfish

seagrass

starfish

coral

limestone

seaweed

stingrays